THE NATURAL LAW
OF WATER

POEMS BY KATHLEEN CULVER

Circledance Books
Melrose, Florida

ISBN 10: 0-9650665-3-3
ISBN 13: 978-0-9650665-3-2

Library of Congress Cataloging-in-Publication Data

Culver Kathleen, 1939-
  The Natural law of water : poems / by Kathleen Culver.
    p. cm.
  ISBN-13: 978-0-9650665-3-2 (pbk.)
  ISBN-10: 0-9650665-3-3 (pbk.)
  I. Title.

  PS3603.U63N38 2007
  811'.6—dc22

                              2007027967

ACKNOWLEDGEMENTS

  A few of these pieces were printed by *Moonseed, Common Lives, Women's
Voices, Santa Fe Review, Bridges,* and underground zines and anthologies.
  I have been given huge gifts of work, wisdom, and encouragement by
Portia Cornell, Barbara Davis, Lynne Kimmel, Joan Larkin, Marj Norris,
Feral Wilcox, Leslita Williams—the first to read binders of my writings
grouped up and visible, come of the caves.
  Others who cheered me on were my mother, Gractia Culver, my brother,
Bob, and my friends—Catherine Turner, Kathy Freeperson, and Jan Hahn.
I would have loved the chance to put the book in their hands.
  Abby Bogomolny of Burning Bush Publications asked me many years ago
for a collection of my poems; that invitation opened the possibility and now
has fulfilled it, in fact, made it a delightful process.
  And finally, a big thanks goes to Jeanne Blethen for the cover photo,
Randi Cameon for the author photo, and Julie Esbjorn of JS Design Studio
for the book design.

TABLE OF CONTENTS

THE NATURAL LAW OF WATER

I. CONFLUENCES

AT FIFTY

Of all of my lovers, whom did I love the most?
I loved all of my lovers the most,
all of my lovers the longest,
because they were all the most beautiful,
and we all asked who
because we were all scared
to say how much we loved
all of us.

The most of all my lovers did I love, and
did I love the most? And did all
of my lovers love the most?
Most of my lovers loved all who did, yes.
All of my lovers loved me and all of my lovers the most.

WHAT YOU HEAR

the voices curl around
each other like erotic vines,
when you can't see the two
it seems clear they are lovers, ah,
but then the lie of the visible,
you see them standing apart, never
making contact, never
making love

but what you hear! the voices
build to crescendos,
story pieces turn by turn get shorter,
phrases dive into each other's sentences
finish each other's thoughts until
they both speak almost at once
a choral reading,
a chant,
a catharsis of one being,
one shout, one
sigh, one silence

POEM IN BLACK AND BROWN

You are not black but brown.
You reach to my cheek with moistened
brown finger to lift the black eyelash
and hold it and then open
your fingers and the black eyelash
is on your beige thumb and you
grin because we know we'll marry.
Your black slacks long-legged,
your black jacket, long arms, black shoes
in the snowy street. Black eyes
wink in your brown face—
At night like Mother Nature
you pull the comforter over our
sleeping earth, and we make love
under silver stars nestling
in the black quilted stitches.

I REMEMBER WHAT DIDN'T HAPPEN

the evening I came to your boat
    leaving my path from work to home
    to step on board into your hand
    under your mast and sail
the night we camped with a group of students
    whom you harangued magnificently
    with tales of the planet's need,
    before you curled beside
    me, into me, under the late stars
I remember what you told me of the time
    you hit the man in the bar, the time
    you hit your brother beside the car,
and I remember what did happen —the sprig of moss,
    your eyes and mine, our walking,
    our voices, the quick touch of my hand to
    your fist wrapped in adhesive and gauze.

SONG

I am the water
turquoise in my heart
purple, labia like, rich

capes to enfold
I am cold, the cold
that awakens you,

after you scream and shudder
after you clench up, holding
yourself back from me

giving as little as possible
until we meet in the same
heat imperative

then you open your strength
and dive under and move
I am the water burst into rainbows

afterwards in the sun, I lie on
your skin alive with
diamond light

THE BUS STATION NIGHT

When we met
your face appeared
and disappeared
behind the post like a
strobe light,
and I danced from side to side
to catch the sight,
and you made a man's overcoat
a witty, daring costume
not showing yourself as you
usually were, but who you were
that moment.
I could see right away
you were quick,
not like your pictures —
better, more quickly changing
than a photograph
in my hand, so I needn't
try to hold you, though
I'd want to, to have you
palm-sized, a frame
around you I could
step into, but I would
bumble and bump, accidentally
interrupt you, yell
in your ear, knock your glass
over, and get you
disappearing and appearing again, dodging me
for real.   Your coat, the jacket I left
hung in the same closet, a month in the dark,
wondering as jackets might, where
we were, and a continent apart,
whether we were a we.

THE CARD

village post office's
        cold rain sets off the pink clitoral
            origami on the card
              I sent you, surely
          the postmistress is tempted
      to reach out and touch
     the gaily flowering shape, and
  surely she knows
seeing me blush
        the same pink,
          seeing the urgency I have
             packaging this card so its petals
                are not crushed.
          seeing me early enough
           to catch the first mail out of town.
       I check my watch
     you are in the air now
   and the card will follow you
  quickly—a part of me, this paper orchid
to thank you

BURNING THE REMAINS

poking at charred love letters
with a stick, a sword, a rapier, she said
be gone, thou devastator
thou torch
song

CURRENTS

Under the bright blue winter sky
over the cold shining water, it's lunch time
after the morning's paddling.

We tie the two canoes together
drift downstream
with the current and the wind.

Avocado slices on rice cakes
tahini sauce,
carob and pears,
figs with almonds inside.

Delicious
our bodies at ease like juicy figs,
our minds clean and crunchy as
the almonds

It's one of those beautiful days
when nothing's safe,
a partner of many years moves focus
to another.

I carefully place a rice cake on a paddle
and pass it to a friend
Someone peels an orange to share.

Under this open sky, on the glittering Suwannee River
with its golden browns and greens and blues, multiple

currents flow with the natural law of water,
and overhead's a sunbow at noon.

A CURSE ON THAT WOMAN

May she win the love of her life and then
May she develop a vicious chronic whistling
   fart so her new lover can't bear to be
   in the same room with her
The scum! —may she take Spanish rice to every potluck
   and may she undercook her rice and
   may partakers look at her first in pity,
   then anger, then may they spit the rice up on her shirt
And may the shirt they spoil
   be the one she has borrowed from
   her boss —may the shirt be an
   heirloom from the boss's sainted grandma'am
   and now be forever streaked with tomato sauce
   and uncooked rice and green bile.
May she, that would-be writer, write only
   out-of-doors in the rain with
   washable ink so her poor poems
   end up in the mud puddles, in the murk they deserve
   and resemble.
May all her underwear get tight
   as the day passes,
May her journal be found
   by her students,
May she watch
   lottery numbers, see her numbers
   come up winners, and then realize she
   shredded her ticket in the dryer.
May she get stuck in the clothes-dryer
   she is trying to retrieve her ticket from
and go round and round
and no one open the door,
and her friends just watch and laugh and
leave her smooshed up against the
glass door like a mad tv

and may I be the one who opens the door
and may she climb out of the dryer and fall on
    her knees to thank me
and have to listen to
    me say
    "You don't deserve life, you
      scum
but I give it to you
for after all, I
am a merciful person."

THIS TIME AROUND

This time around I want a lover who plays
a little hard to get, not one who crawls
into my lap before I say hello,
not regular as the sun. I want a moon lover,
changing from the beginning.

This time I don't want adrenalin to surge up my arm
as I reach for the phone, and I don't want us
to read newspapers to each other in late breakfasts
beside the lake, no buttered toast and coffee, no
orange marmalade. I don't want to be too excited
or too secure.

This time I want a lover who likes a moonrise, but
you know, can take it or leave it,
who doesn't obsess about it and make me sit waiting
staring raw-eyed at a horizon
amidst mosquitoes, for hours.

This time I want a lover who knows how
to let go, who doesn't try to hang on after
the passion has quieted, who does the end
as well as the beginning.

This time I want to know it won't last; I don't want
to like her so much. I don't want to resist
the process so much. I don't want to lose my faith
so much, that each turn is equal
blessing.

FIRST MORNING

The storks in knock-kneed strut parade
across the road, a good sign you say. You found
this place earlier in a moment
of magic when your hair was dirty, your
mind tangled and you wanted a shower.

Hair still wet, you draw me from the rest
of the peace-walkers, here to show off your oasis,
the boardwalk, handy showers for a quarter,
ten campsites and four manatees.

The birds strut in groups, easily
stopping cars on the park road. We imagine ourselves
in each tent site—here we have shade, here most
privacy, here we are nearest to the wooden dock
with manatees to see.

As though your morning's still-wet hair
is usual, and the smell of shower on your neck,
as though we ever before had planned a place to sleep
together, we are gay and nonchalant as birds,
knowing everything will stop for us.

II. MIRRORING

MOONSONG

She brought the moon
she brought the moon,
she brought the moon,
to me, to my window, with her finger,
reached inside, opened latches,
opened shutters, opened curtains,
let the light in, took the night back,
sweet black darkness, silver moonshine,
made my heart shine.

She was a rover,
took me over,
over mountains,
over cities,
flying over,
took me over, over.

And I would sail her,
trim her sheets tight,
lift her onto her own bow wave,
wing and wing and winds to fly her.
We were lovers,
night watchers,
sea reachers,
star sailors,
miles of solitude between us
brought no meadow days to ease us;
when the moon and tides were fullest
only then she'd come to see me.

But when her shadow passed my window
then she brought the moon
to me;
she brought the moon
she brought the moon
she brought the moon
to me.

THE GIRL I LEFT BEHIND

In those days, I was always forgetting something.
I tried to remember everything, but I'd leave
something behind, forget some thing, forget
about what others thought was right,
forget the colors appropriate for the seasons.
For instance, that trip to Paducah for a luncheon. The silk
sleeves on my beautiful pink dress were
too long for spring, said Lanie Dyer, rich
Lanie Dyer. Oh my pride, for sure I would
leave that behind next time. This I thought as I broke
off the brittle pink sleeves on the shrimp Lanie
Dyer had told us we each might have eight of.
I had had high hopes, but then I was bare shame.

I needed a cover-up, so I went
to my aunt's card table with a scarf
on my head because my curls might fall down
in the damp. They tried to pry that
scarf off me, but I played bridge with those adults
looking as though I were on an Ellis Island ferry, armored
for my first game in a hostile new land.
I had left the old country behind.

Then I learned to leave my face behind. That seemed to be
the best way since I would never have the right clothes,
the right hair, but would try to, though the hope for
success was behind like the gulls screaming behind
the ferry looking for scraps, for fish caught in eddies.
Leaving the face made things easier, no one could
recognize me; it wasn't me. From then on
disguise was elementary, leaving out
certain words, leaving out my name, leaving out
whom I loved, leaving out where I lived,
leaving my mother, my father, my home, no one
could find me.

In the dance my foot was not there
In the talk my tongue was not there
In how I rode, the swaying seat was
not there. I went far away, so far, shame forgot
to look for me; finally.
I so outdistanced shame
that I at last forgot to hide. And somehow then,
parts came back. One day my tongue came
singing up the steps,
one day my jeans legs kicked a dress
off the porch and sat on the swing,
and the swing I rode swayed back and forth
so easy, I forgot I had ever forgotten how
to do it. And my hips rocked and I opened,
and my names gathered around and came back,
and the loves I'd disowned came back.
And the pot of sugar snap peas I had picked and had shelled
in my lap rang a song of good food
I'd known and forgotten I'd liked.
Of course my hair grew back. And my voice
returned, and now we go everywhere together,
leaving only
the scarves, the skirts, or sleeves,
leaving only the coverings behind.

SESTINA FOR A WITCH

Past the door and trees she stares into the moon,
in her hand holding a piece of wood
that she will carve into a banjo
neck; she whittles off the nubs of sweet gum
hardened in the frost,
tosses golden beads and shavings through the doorway.

Her movement makes the yellow doorway
blink shut like an owl's eye, like a new moon.
Another movement: on the white crisp frost —
like footsteps of some spirits in the wood —
dancing shadows of the leaves of sweet gum
move in time as though they heard from other spheres, a banjo.

She teaches herself to play the banjo
tunes by harkening to the breezes in her doorway;
picks out tunes in ancient modal scales, sucked sweet gum
sings songs for different phases of the moon,
echoes insects chatting in the woods
hears, reflects, keeps windows open far beyond the frost.

She gives a stiff-kneed curtsy to the frost,
makes icicle tones for it on the banjo
when freezes burn the summer green to blackened woods,
allows that cold right in her doorway,
cold that comes a long way over the wire grass from snowy moon
through the star-shaped leaves of sweet gum.

Liquidamber —botanists' name for the sweet gum
oozes from the tree, hardens to amber rock in the frost,
melts in sun, shines in full moon,
makes topaz beads of sweat on straining neck of banjo.
She plays, and using the frailing fingers as their doorway,
tunes of crows and towhees fly in from the woods.

Here's the mandolin sound, a chip-o-willow in the woods
and owls, who. . .who. . . who-who, from the gum
root swamp. A frog leaps across a doorway.
Howdy! Are you a princess running from the frost?
Leave your crown behind and listen to my banjo;
welcome, sit with me, and watch the moon.

CHERIE

boundaries that work for others didn't work for Cherie
most of us hesitate to hug people and hold people
we haven't known long
most of us say I love you to only a few people
so when Cherie was giving us long hugs, at first
we thought it a little overboard
but we got used to it
and grew to want that welcome place
in her arms snuggled up to her big warm body.

most of us are super careful not to walk around
with fly open or to be caught by the U.P.S.
at home with no clothes on, our 40 D's swinging in the breeze,
but she wasn't worried, her famed sarong slipped open sometimes
for a second in public places. lordess! Cindy said "if you don't
learn to tie your
sarong, you'll get all of us arrested"

Cherie was the queen of flexible
no rules
it wasn't easy doing contracts and arrangements with Cherie
last week's agreements didn't wall her in
we're neighbors she'd say explaining the migration of my tools and
clothes and favorite cups to her house
we're neighbors and
that explained everything

it was easy to love her at the same time
you were shaking your head exasperated
now she's not here
and I want her here
who cares if my teacups move to her house
or if she does the laundry in the middle of the night
and keeps me awake
and then leaves the clothes in the washer for days
or gives my ratty old sleeping bag to someone who needs it more
than I do

come back
boundaries don't hold you
I know you went right through
that hard ground that line of death
to another plane
I know you can come back to us when our
hardened ways and walls need melting

Cherie McArthur 1956-2005

SHOPPING BAG WOMAN

Solemn woman with one eye drooping
Walking past the bowed and weathered stoop
Black dust on the street
Black dust on her cheek

The handle cord of wound
Paper tears at the crowd's
Pushing, it will not last
The block's length she passes.

She hears a squirrel skittering,
A pigeon coo and flutter
A friend bending a sycamore
The clang and sigh of semi brakes

Jack hammer, shovel, her shuffle,
Pinpoint of blue, a hand she takes,
Broken carnations underfoot
The quaking shudder of subway.

ISIS AGAIN AT THE WAFFLE HOUSE

I return to thee oh mother once again
Oh Isis of ten thousand breasts, even at the awful house,
For strangers on the road, you're always here
The known touch, the plastic menu, and welcome in
Your familiar voice.

All waitresses are you, are goddess
Deep Georgia drawls, the snapping hurry ups
The milk, the cream for coffee
The kind words for all us skunks and skinks
For queers and queries.

You will make fresh decaf and chili, tell us all
About the latest accident on the interstate
The progress of a police chase as you observe it easily from
Where you stand and we, mere mortals,
Crane our necks to see.

Here in the waffle house leaning against our orange
Padded seat backs, under the lineup of white globes
Like planets in an orderly solar system, auspicious
Planetary influences, we find bits of good news in the paper
Look curiously at a fellow worshipper the next booth over.

We are secure here, taking shelter with you, Isis
With the delicious and dangerous grease
That makes food go down easy. Oh! The sight of your
Red fingernails peeking through handfuls of green dill pickles
They're rubies, amulets you give us for safe travel.

THE ACCOUNTING

She purred and across the slick boardroom table she dealt out
pads of paper like playing cards. One slid to the edge and teetered
gracefully like Fred Astaire who after a moment of suspense would
catch his balance and his partner.

A large red-hot emerged between her teeth, an eyeball staring at
us. Iced pitchers of water, spaced down the table, failed to cool her
auditors. She snapped her pointer across her palm, and smiled:
"I've looked forward to this meeting."

She bit down on the red-hot and flames spurted from her mouth.
"I know we all want a more effective organization." She spoke in
separated syllables.

Beads of sweat appeared on the pitchers and our foreheads.

"Who would like to speak first?"

PULL DOWN MENU

she opened the refrigerator
and found a stack of envelopes
and letterhead not lettuce head
she set a leaf flat upon a plate
where ink could spread like
octopus blood.
fine with her, she didn't care
for vegetarian poems.
she lifted the ink out of the door
poured it on a sheet of raw paper
and ate.

BREAKS
(SOME OF THE LINE BRAKES MAY BE IN ERROR
BUT I BRAKE FOR BREATH)

foot crumbled flack jack model
Marjorie so pleasantly
pierced the padding
with a splinter
marvelous said Stuart grabbing
the curtain into
a toga, had I known
the basic government, that is the
recipe, I'd simmer olive bats? hats? hots?
for everyone, peace on low power
peas train chewed clackety clack
teeth, loose, slacker happy let
s make yackety yack. Got them
stingy hinges bending, ululating universe
ooze now, a pillow blows frilly feathers
for a garage sail and entropy wind winds
down true grits lose all wore out war close.

THE MUSE MAKES A HOUSE CALL

There is this duck in my head that quacks,
block, block.
There is a pill that is bitter,
swill, swill.
Where is the will that is better,
till, till?
There is this quack at my desk that sits back.

The muse arrives
in a great coat of earth,
grave as a grave,
massive in girth,

She extracts a bone,
sips a teaspoon of blood,
"Umm, savory, my dear,
quite good."

There is the quick in your foot that jumps up,
Dance, dance.
There is the thorn in the thigh —
Snag, snag.
There is the tale of the tree —
Hag, hag.
There is this wake in the world that stings —
alive, alive.
There is this dread of the Voice —
Lies, lies.
There is this fear of the muse's surprise.

"Now heat up those bones, chew them like scones.
Brew up those tears for a tea.
You'll do very well indeed.
I'll be going now. To you, Godspeed."

MARGARET AND THE GROUNDSKEEPER

Margaret
liked her hedgerow
thick with hiding places
spontaneous
bird bursts
poisonous berries
weed blossoms.

I wanted to trim the hedge, so she could see
more sky, like a heaven,
and she said, well okay, then,
at least then it won't scratch
the neighbor's car.
But let the yard mostly stay
wild and willful, she laughed.
Let me see the nests wedged
in thicket and bramble some more
let that family of skunks think we don't see them
sneaking by under the bushes, the family line,
in their dressed up
white and black parade.

She humored me, knowing I needed
to feel I could comfort her,
me with my snippers and clippers
and notions of heaven and blue skies where
she'd go when she died; she didn't
let on she could see me worrying
or that there in the thistles and prickles
and scratchy skunk fumes, her heaven
had already started.

BIZARRE HOW THE LOVELIEST

sight in all christendom is
called devil's den.

I'm sure it's because when
you swim in August in the cold

pure water, against the
current, the force of the flow

from deep in the earth, when you reach
hands outstretched to get over

the drop off where the white underwater
cliffs open to the green, violet, chasm

with the blue diamond at the center,
and you feeling like you're flying

over the transparent water, and the beauty
shocks just as much as the cold,

you keep swimming hard, to hold on to the
sight of that deep blue cave because it feels like

an ancient oracle is telling you something
if you can just

hang on, something pagan, something
from the earth herself.

III. CROSS-CURRENTS

VIETNAM

Just when I think the shoulder pain is gone,
the feeling comes back again.
When green fields in Vietnam sleep in peace,
a land mind blows up.

The feeling comes back —
I still cry in the night for my mother;
An old land mine blows up,
Rudy, you old communist, you're dead now, but you were dead right.

I cry in the night for my mother still;
I'm not a sad person.
Rudy, you old communist, you're dead now but you were dead right —
That war was built on lies.

I'm not a sad person,
I protest and crack jokes, march with peace signs.
We knew that war was built on lies —
slick talk, an oil slick, all comes back again.

We protest, have hope, march with peace signs
Lest the ease we live in make its own quagmire.
And slick talk, an oil slick, all comes back again.
Vietnamese monks set themselves on fire;

The easy life makes its own quagmire.
Curl of fetal position praying for a new turn,
Vietnamese monks set themselves on fire—
Beside the mines, now, unfurl green ferns.

THE NIGHT THE WAR BEGAN

It is 64 degrees in Gainesville, Florida, spring-like, but
   34 degrees in Baghdad, where a light frost
   offers its own crystalline geometries to the green and red tiles
by the mosques.

Oh so cool and quiet, not many left in town.
     The people in Baghdad deliberate
leaving the city. One woman says, "I think
the bombs will come tonight, at 3:00, in the new moon
when it is darkest." Another says, "No, I
    think the Americans will wait
       till we are relaxed, when our
guard is down."

Buses fill to bursting—Iraqi people
    with bags, baggage:
       "Shall we take our pictures, our jewels:" No,
it will be over soon. We will go to our relatives
in the country, and then we'll come back."
    They pull scarves around their heads and shoulders.
If it must happen, let it be tonight, one woman thinks,
looking out the bus window.

It is 64 in Florida. In one house roommates
    mill about the communal area,
wanting to be together, create
    a new space for eating
    in front of the television;
    Indian rug, lamp, table, are donated from the bedrooms.
"It looks terrific in here," someone says, waking
from a nap to find the changed room.
People in Baghdad are rearranging things too.

A shopkeeper in a light jacket
              stands outside his shop X-ing his
windows with tape, looking up to the sky. "It may be tonight,"
              he says, "I hear the Americans
              like to fight under the cover
              of darkness." Everything
is happening according to the plan, schedules and maps,
neatly arranged. News coverage cleaned and polished.

In Gainesville, the three roommates light candles and
              for the first time, make a meal together—
                        millet and tofu, broccoli,
                        bits of seaweed.
"I like this seaweed," says one, surprised. "Not me,"
              says another; they finish
                        eating and turn on the evening news
tense with the possibility of war.

On the television a map of Baghdad is shown.
The river Tigris winds through the center.
                        "Tigris, such a holy-sounding name."
"It's from the Bible," says one roommate, a Baptist.
"Isn't that where higher mathematics began?"
              asks the engineering student, and "Isn't that
                        where the great matriarchies began?"
asks the English major.

In Baghdad the journalists remark that the sky
              has suddenly filled with light.
"Like fireworks," they say.
One journalist's face twists, holding back something,

who knows what? Expression of excitement or horror?
                        In Florida , tears run down the cheeks of one
              roommate sitting on the edge of the couch,
leaning toward the television.

Another roommate returns from the kitchen
           to find a war has started.
                    "They're sick," she screams.
The third roommate thinks of Nixon who
Used a TV appearance to announce the very moment
                    of U.S. troops crossing the river
into Cambodia.
"Meeting the deadline," is the phrase used
           in both wars, each beginning
                    with similarly perfect timing, exactly
in the middle of the evening meal,
in the middle of the evening news.

In Florida tonight the temperature is balmy, but in
           Baghdad it is 34 and a light frost
                    lands its delicate geometries on the house,
along the river, on the mosques, amidst the bombs.

MOVIE STILLS

the preacher in a white collar
face striped with blood and dismay
not at his injury, but at their violence

the marine getting his wings pinned into his flesh
his eyes looked like they wanted to ask a question before
they closed and he passed out from pain

the young woman walking into the segregated bus station
head steady, eyes glancing from side to side,
facing hate, possibly death

another face when the gunshot
severed the moment, he's
prescient, poised, listening

a peace demonstrator thrown
to the pavement, remembering not to fight, keeping
an interior balance

HOW CHRISTIANITY GOT STARTED

Since I've canceled my morning newspaper,
I look out the window and instead of the Sunday news
read my palm, that is, the palm tree
across the neighbor's fence, each frond wide as the palm of a hand
of a giantess, a yard across, with fifteen long thin fingers
that curve toward the ground, become a shimmering hula skirt
inviting us to dance to the ukulele music of the earth
(thus, the travel and the arts sections).
Some fingers point up, catching sunlight along their blades,
swords of light ready for a battle of ideas
(editorial page, shall we say?)
The huge fringed leaf, like a newspaper held open,
a newspaper with only good news, lifted by a strong arcing arm.
Palms! —now I remember, Palm Sunday —of course, perfect
for the triumphal procession of Jesus to Jerusalem.

Makes me think of Jesus as a southern sort of Jewish fellow
one well-acquainted with the dry clatter of palm fronds.
How maybe one morning he put down his newspaper and stared
at these mammoth green fans, larger than life,
(more magnificent than the smaller versions he'd seen
in pots in hotel lobbies). These great green hands
translate light to give us our oxygen, our breath,
breath which we take in and transform,
and give back. Jesus pondered and gasped.
We are all sifters of glory —all transmitters
of great circles of energy.

It's like infield practice (Jesus had this vision
though he did not play baseball himself).
Here is the sports page
catching, throwing, transmitting, transforming
 —we're all in a divine loop.

Here is the real Sunday news, here is the
Sunday list of lotteries we have won —
the palms, these great broom rakes gathering
up sky for us to breathe. And Jesus thought,
"I'm going to lay down my paper
and start a religion." So he did.

THE CLOCK SHOP

Floor clocks, door clocks, wall clocks,
hall clocks, all the clocks ticking.

Body clock ticking, that's the ticker,
that's the heart, that's the ticket.
Take a fat chance, and do the hat dance.

Biological clock ticking,
had ticked, has ticked, have
kids, be a wiz. Can't tick, frantic!

Economic clock ticking,
working on the job —hard
putting in the time card,
get money, spend money,
save money, crave money.

Politic-ticking
metronome, methadone,
peace and justice, end war,
love more, name a star.

And the spiritual
clock ticking, for the mission, what mission?
Get a mission. Keep in
shape for the mission.

Oh the earth clock's ticking.
Thank heavens. Thank earth.
Recycle, Rock!
Hands on the clock turning cartwheels.
Oh clock shop, all the pendulums swaying,
sounding on the hour.

Birds popping out to say, it's eight, celebrate!
The ticking and humming...the timing, the chiming,
light is a glinting and a glittering on the glass faces.
Do it! Do it! Wind up and swing, wind up and sing!
It's the best
shop on the street, it's the watch shop,
it's the time trip, it's the clock shop.

HOW THE FUTURE USED TO LOOK

A fine shining place, a place of libraries,
red and green stained glass windows and deep chairs,
shelves full of classic literature, the word played on a cello

Words would be eyeglasses to make the world easier to see.
The speakers might pass away but the words wouldn't. Books:

Would always be there, old souls ready to nourish young souls,
like the old moon holding the new moon,
clay pots filled with rich dirt and seeds, ready to grow roses,
thistles, and potatoes.

Holding in our hands a Hopkins or a Dickinson, we'd know
every good poet would find audience, even if
only a shard, a jagged cup perfect for Sappho's lovely word.

Time and readers would sort out the practice sessions like the
outer leaves of artichokes, and under the bristles
the good hearts would always be found.

Outside the library the art of life would thrive, moments
always evolving, consciousness more Aquarian, just peace,
human honed to angel. The scarce pennies of the day
didn't matter, weren't a worry; our future would be
rich, right on.

That's what we looked forward to, we children who
checked out four books at the library
each Saturday, and then headed to the movies,
we who grew up in the great age of musical comedy,
we who sang in the rain and tap-danced in rain puddles.

LUNCH HOUR

mercury at my feet rises
on blistering pavements
winged and demented I
window-shop with the glad guilt
of a safecracker

who can arrest this heated
mind, fogging prim furniture
store windows, denuding dusty
trusses

the bare feet the tender toes
portage over rock and hedge
the lunch break the
jail break

I write graffiti with my fingertip
on a sunburned body
prone in the park
the words vanish suddenly
without evidence

I hear the loan sharks standing
on their doorway soap boxes:
repent of materiality

I receive the propositions of gum machines
and sidewalk parking meters, infamous and
flirtatious

blessings be to this music
of siren and mobs
take armfuls of daisies
from flower stands
present them to winos

GLOBAL WARMING—THE BRIGHT SIDE

The waters of Lochloosa and
Cross Creek are rising
over the road. Maybe
we should just let the
cars sink into the swamp
forever. Why not? They're
kayaking across
the prairie. Anything can
happen.

MY COUNTRY 'TIS OF THEE

Trying to decide
what to pack
maybe in an overnight bag,
the Bill of Rights
the Constitution
and in a trunk,
WPA lodges, hewn beams, huge stones,
rustic American architecture
built by the federal government
for jobs in the depression,
places regular people can still afford.

Looking around at the piles in my room,
I see banjo music,
trout streams,
all over the bed, the floor,
so much I'd like to keep—
organic gardens, fat funny looking carrots,
and freedom—that's got to go in.

But a refugee can't carry much.
Maybe others will bring
things we can share, to
wherever it is we
try to set up camp,
try to start America all over again.

IV. SOURCE

PERSONAL AD FROM THE EARTH

4 1/2 Billion-year-old planet seeks highly conscious species for
life-long romantic partnership. Hoping to share interest in
overseeing complex organization of life forms, chemical and physical
interactions, a family enterprise including everything from rocks
to microbes, crops to cybernetics. After work we'd play—moon-
lit nights swimming with phosphorescent dolphins, sun-filled
mornings on wind-swept prairies. I'm a planet made for adventure,
sensuousness, poetry, ready to give my all to a species who can join
me and return my love. My last partnership ended in heartbreak,
but I still hope to find the right species someday. If you enjoy
turquoise waters and fresh air, give me a call.

THE LAKE

Simply a surface,
yet we gathered,

the squawking blackbirds
dashing about,

the bicyclists who stopped
in brief awe.

The tall fluffed phragmites reed
seemed to come from Egypt,

tossed its tassels at us. The lake
lay like a flat gray stone

a stone thrown in the marshes
with writing on it that

moved, a live hieroglyphic;
I held my soul toward it

asking for a blessing, a word,
a spray of water drops.

SPRING FLOOD

The black river deceptively quiet, high enough
in its banks to hide most rocks.

No comforting v's for the canoe to slide into
for safe passage, but

current fast enough to deliver a dog into
an alligator's mouth.

The cypress knees gather around the mother like
monks.

I tiptoe amongst them so as not to disturb their
meditations.

I add to the quiet
with my partial deafness.

BEES

    spring pries a door open —finds
a window crack it can get through
sprouts need to grow
push up get more space
spring needs to go on a trip
feel faraway new
blossoms need lots of light
and wiggle room
and audiences; spring
needs
audiences
   spring winds need dry leaves
to blow loose, need tiny leaves
to pull into being big
spring winds need to be heard
need to howl loud
whisper in your ear
to tickle your skin till you're
full of desire
spring winds need to caress you nude
give you lots of sun, and take
more for themselves
   spring opens doors, throws away keys
calls from the center of every flower
blissed-out bees
welcome everywhere

MORNING LEAPT

across
the fence of the horizon
ran into the field
uncurling wound leaves
popping open umbrella blooms
chickweed, portulaca
red sorrel and dandelion
whooping it up

breathing hard and happy
morning finally flung herself
on the grass full of flowers
soaking in her own noon sun

TUBER GETS RELIGION

The water that springs
out of the good-humored sandboils,
out of the deep turquoise rock hollows
can't be got at the souvenir stand.

The blue gray green molten glass pouring forth purity
can't be put in a bucket; you've got to go to the source
where endless infinite miraculous is usual,
sign and shrine of the good strong heart of nature.

Exuberant prayer
laughing with the water
touched by the gnarled
fingers of cypress,

the essence of earth and us,
central fountain unfolding,
opening her aquifer grand as an opera
put another nickel in for some swelling fine music,

multicolored bank chuckling and blinking like
an old fashioned cathedral shaped
jukebox —
guardian spirit, clown face of light.

DRIVE

through the open
fields and woods through the gum root
swamp. nothing could stop me, barbed wire
fence, creeks, hammocks of palmetto, oak
and vines too thick for a quark to pass
through, no bed could rest me, i drove past
friends' homes on the lake looking for a
late night party, i cut through curves on
the winding road. the domesticated cows
and horses were looking at me like i was
crazy . . . and i was . . . looking for a
light on—nothing—then at my cabin as i
got out of the car and foot hit the pine
needles on the sand under the stars, i
heard the phone ringing in my house,
crashed through the dark to get to it, and
heard your voice crazed as mine. why did
you go back out there, you said, i wanted
to sleep with you. . . you did? i've won the
lottery, a butterfly has landed on my hand,
my swamp honda becomes winged again...
i'll be there i say, over field and hill in a
flash. I will turn around and go back.
i will arrive a five-banjo jig, in a
red velvet cape, you're wild you say, let me
drive this time. but i think you can't make it over
the streams and through the barbed wire.
let's just see each other tomorrow i say.
I hang up, howl again and go to bed to
lie awake and listen to the chuckwills willow sing.

SONG OF THE BLOOD

Beating pulse of the blood,
thrum on the belly on the slit drum,
rhythm carve a path into the cave,
the core,
the burning pit inside
the cool pool of creation.

Cracked bone booming,
speak tree now,
tree spirit, speak through the
drum, pulling your voice
from my palms.
I receive your sounds
in my arms.

O hold me as I disintegrate,
as I fly into pieces
joyful, one moment that is eternity
one moment that is everywhere.

My eyes roll, seeing all over the earth,
like a sun, spirit transparent,
holding the planet,
its seas. I am aching with this stretching.

My knees reach around a mountain,
I rub the furry trees against my fur,
I am insatiable I am starving,
stars fold on me like burning rain drops.
I am not in pain.

I spin I do huge trunk rolls with my torso
continents are my breasts, my abdomen
chunks a new continent into being.
Gaia, Gaia your rivers,
my blood.

LEAVES

fall waters fall, the sap pulls back,
rains flood the woods and roads
moisture within the leaf flares before it
dries, i dream two lovers
going back and forth and hurting both,
this tree that tree, in love here, so bright,
in love there, so bright,
it's all over in a few weeks

and we are left bare

and there are no passions permitted
for any of us. birds leave the dark
wet branches, no quickening
of breath, no song, no obsession.
no rivals no jealousy no comparisons
no yearning, no illumination. gone
the bright colors that unbutton the
blouse and kiss the breasts
and heart

MOOD MAROON

Blood sitting quiet now, very slowly turning
maroon, a marriage of red and blue,
dark blood at the end of menses.
I am here where I didn't expect to be,
no way out visible, and it's time to get going.
The sunset trims clouds with maroon.
Marooned sounds like doomed, left to die,
an inaction that suggests action,
isolated in a blue swamp of alligators,
in a subtropic November where sweet gum leaves
never get bright red. Japanese maples.
The sweater that hangs alone and never
seems to match anything. You funny bird,
you, like a purple gallinule that hides and calls out
from its hiding place.

JEEP RIDE IN FLORIDA

In the swamp, the cypress and oak forest stands in water
and reflections of the trees, moves like boiling linguini
like zebras and leopards striped and speckled with light.
Our narrow road on the dike overlooks
owls and fish swimming in the reflections
of our submarine jeep. As we are wiggled
and jounced deeper into the wet circus of the woods,
we see ourselves down there, looking up
trying to fathom the goofy world above.

TWO GODDESSES: A CHILDREN'S SONG

Yours are the swamps, the frogs in the stumps
the bites on the fingers
the splinters in rumps.

      Ah, yet yours are the fairy, the fleeting, the fine
      the frost-flowers in morning,
      filigree vine.

But yours are fiddle tunes lost in the forest
the caves with quick bats
the chuckling bug chorus.

      So I get to sit on a sunbeam thin
And I get to ride the wild dragons within.

      And at day or at night when our paths cross again,
We'll each tell the stories of worlds where we've been.

V. TRANSITS

CARMINE STREET SUMMER: GREENWICH VILLAGE

All new to me, the black and white tiles
in the entranceway, where you, city-wise,
taught me to have my keys out with
one key ready to stab an eye of any mugger.
Then past the harlequin floor. You said,
don't relax, one door behind.
one to go.

Now hi to the pet roaches rushing out to greet us. You turned on
lights with your laughing,
Kathy, you with a Marlene-Dietrich-with-a-cold voice
singing falling in love again. When our friend Nancy
had a dream about a baby elephant named George, with
a low growling smoky voice, I knew it was you,
you, the beauty, the singer, tomboy Ava Gardner
with wide cheekbones, you, pointing your finger in the air
to accent the words, we could hear the jazz, you were sexy
show biz.

You would say hoarsely, hey Kathleen, from
the bed which had no box springs just a mattress
on the floor and a headboard and a wooden frame around it.
I'd climb over and down and we'd have a kiss while
Todd Rundgren was singing, hitting high falsettos that
would fly over the percussion sounds of truck traffic
in the street outside like sweet baby
angels.

Give me one more victory I'll be on my way.
This prayer was a song of the summer, my only New York
summer, the Rock the Boat Baby summer, the B and C's bar
summer when lipstick lesbians would come in from
Long Island and sometimes pick one of us up for the night
and that was okay with me and okay
with you.

(WO)MAN'S BEST COMPANION

Reading a comic book while she
walks down the street with S.W.
Cool Dog who pulls hard at the leash:
don't read, look —a pumpkin sandwich,
it's Halloween, the veil is thin.

Snuffle Woof Cool Dog, at first she says,
the dead, who cares?
But then she remembers
all her other canine walking partners gone,
My Stash, Lunge, Buddy, Lord Cedric.

Snuffle Woof, can you feel your ancestors
within you? She thinks of them all,
which one liked comic books,
which one ate pumpkin,
which one ate the leash—

Yes, I'll put away my comic book,
take me away puppy love, my heart's
got heartburn from eating at
Taco Bell, take me away, Snuffle
Woof, my own.

LEAVING THE CITY

With the San Francisco beats drumming on eardrums,
we rolled north from Maud's and the Fillmore auditorium
rolled up the highway to Mendocino, hearing
bass fiddle thump of tire on tarmac
turning wine time to wind drinking, turning
plain Jane to Redwing, Oceanlight, Circledance,
coastal country dykes, growing borage flowers for salads,
growing beards, climbing among the rocks in the ocean to
gather seaweed—Nori, Fucus, Wakame—
easing into icy water, sometimes black-suited like seals,
sometimes bareskinned, heated from sweat lodges,
listening to the tuba slurping sound of swimming shoes,
to rattles shaking seeds and bones, and chanting.

Fionna, the white light of the moon, mandala,
the dance of the all

We soaked our paychecks in the sea,
the insipid ink of chevron, city hall, facts and figures
—floated away.
We were a hootenanny of hermits with no return addresses

We roamed countryside still dotted with rock and sheep,
the curly tracks of the clouds our signs in the sky.
We were legendary not outlaws but out-of-the-laws,
making books of wilderness words, serving tea to otters who
dropped by at noon to sun their chilly sides.

ANXIETY

The floor seems to move
the vending machine denies you chocolate and gives you
a Payday
the hair dryer fumes
breakfast majorettes twirl in your stomach
a grave opens
bubbles on the puddles stare at you
palms hyper-hydrate
doors stick, keys disappear
every highway lane has eighteen wheelers ahead and behind
you can't remember your address
your phone number, your mother's love,
your connection to a higher power
you step on your own shoelaces.   All so slowly
mind springs loose.

BLACKOUT

we call it mad dog
the good exit
seizure salad wipeout
bolt of voltage

after dream lines
broke under branches
in the storm and flailed
about writing neon

signs on sky
we charge our
part, years of
cataracts released

a lottery win of wonder—
while fed up
friends zip suitcases
leave tight-lipped

we swim down the
empty street under singing
streams of consciousness
cool moon sailing

CLOSE ENOUGH

I couldn't follow your line of thought
but I didn't want to say anything.
Maybe I didn't want to hear it all again,

or maybe I really heard the words and
immediately
erased them. Maybe I
didn't want to un-suppress the memory.

What parts I guessed at of what I heard
had long teeth,
a room was on fire,

someone was gasping, the screams were
subliminal, sound waves above the frequency
I can hear,

the parts hardest to understand —
torn and gaping
too incomplete for a true agony —

little pieces that had exploded,
floated and landed throughout the day
in the yard on the picnic on my skin.

SOUTH CENTRAL FIRES

we paddled in classic fashion on our knees
till this transcontinental connection that could have
sounded like ground travel, train tracks, click clack analysis,
separation, instead was fluid fusion, alchemy,
a determination in her/him and myself combined to make us

partners in canoeing, the river paralleled and then joined
a street of burnt-out businesses, a car shop with two bays,
a clothing boutique s/he laughed, where melted metal hulls
lay limply over steel beams like Dali watches,
dresses over arms of clerks

the choice of route, a compromise, of course, s/he with hair
so short it was a ritual, a costume, elegant arrogant hair yet
curiously vulnerable said the editor. I said s/he wanted to go
down the coast, manatees could be touched with bare hands
perhaps lips, yes, but not yet I said, asserting myself

first the urban run, first liquor stores where liquid poured from
exploded glass, where water lowed over the streets on heads
in cans, in yellow streams, the paddle could crack a
window, just as easily as it slit the glassy water, just as
smooth an entry as a key in the door

on our knees we leaned against the struts, through fog
rising off the water like smoke from ruins, like cathedral
incense, at first barely able
to see cypress trees or traffic till sun burnt off the
morning mist and the journey had become a prayer

DUMPSTERHOME

lost somewhere along some highway
probably clues at mcdonalds bouncing in
the tent, probably clues at wal-mart
twirling in the floor-waxer at 1:00 a.m.,
probably in some of the best dumpsters
the not really clean ones but almost
where piano boxes are folded up and styrofoam
stuffing holds the weary soul being mailed
to rem cycles, hopefully not broken or mangled
always note these particular dumpsters always
touch the phones to check for change, always inhale the last fumes
and rub a little lotion in the skin watch it watch for it what a
downpour in an earthquake a little dandelion green a little
woodslot with pineneedles a curious eye an open hand

TRUCK ERRANDS AT SUNSET

One of the roommates is learning Spanish
ola, boca, bella she chatters,
suddenly the three are quiet

They pass a woman
standing motionless
beside the road

Clearly she came out of
a shaded trailer park
to the highway

To see the sunset.
her cotton dress,
her face, her long hair

Her bare legs
her arms all glowing
in the light, the painless flame

Ola, bella, bella,
ay maria,
whisper the three

FALL FESTIVAL

When markets become satiated with
goods no one wants and
merchandise heaps in hills, and smuggled
cigarettes stain fingers, and phosphoric acid curdles
streams and stomachs with coca cola,
then tropical storms rain inches of grass
carpet and give shawls of bright green
moss, then the hermit sews a rag
with un-matching threads and
selects a sprig of watercress
growing beside the wet ditch
to set upon her rice.

Hear oh wisdom hear the coming wind
of winter, curious and restive,
poking around in barns with
sticks, trying to close doors wedged in
dirt and thickets of weed. Surely
it's festival time, with stray plastic
bags suddenly given life by the
fall wind, and dark decaying
leaves somersaulting down the
streets leftovers from cow trails
and deer paths and magnetic star
scripts. Our raincoats
flutter ceremonially before
they're pulled and tied, hoods lift
to cover ears and faces in
penitence and solitude.

FIRE CIRCLE
South Africa

The old woman trudges for days. She sees
mostly her feet, placing them on switchbacks
cut in early summer by...some young one,
full of glory, bounding, where the old woman
now often needs to stop, to slow her breath down,
to slow her heart down, sleep an hour.
The fourth day she reaches a plateau overlooking
valleys and osseous ridges. You buzzards are
way too early. I know I'll have weeks of peace here.
She hangs her hammocks and gathers
grey rocks for a fire circle.

GARE DU NORD

At first like a cat tiptoeing over wet lawn, she touched
Paris gingerly, angrily, let go the wet railing
quickly, rubbed her hand against her coat
as though fearing germs, as though afraid of
cold water, or of the cold sweat of a stranger.

She took only brief looks in shop windows,
refusing to be seduced,
terse in her requests to shopkeepers:
"*J'ai besoin chapeau de pluie.*"
But seeing the blank look on the clerk,
she wondered if she had actually said
as she intended, "I need a rain hat," or if she
had said, "I need a new head," or,
"My head cries under my hat,"
and she left the shop bareheaded, embarrassed
not to have the language yet to be so exposed.
And later, at a café—watching the
surface of her coffee, she thought,
"I want to have my shoulders back—
joyous to be in this city, but instead
I turn it down, glaring at this bitter mirror
destroying it with a tiny spoon."

Then at the *Gare du Nord* pleading for a ticket
home, she realized the agents did not understand her;
instead they gave her a ticket
to homelessness, to Goya,
a new twist in the twisted faces.
She began to laugh, to
hallucinate keepsakes plastered on the wall,
to hear what was left of that photograph
blow a muted trumpet till Greenwich
lost track of time. Metal against metal
sang, "Who needs you?"

Trains spewed and coughed;
someone selling biscuits screamed
in some language, "Lady,
move your briefcase!" She
understood *la langue* now. File
folders flew through the station
like butterflies.

TANGIERS

Goddesses arrive when
lovers leave so
thank heaven
after having lost
arms to hang onto
necks to obsess on,
when loneliness fills the air,
the goddesses come,
like the breathing of each of us
at separate tables,
like music
sculpted by the bricks we lean against.
Images of monumental she-roes
push out through walls
and though textured by cement,
tortured by culture,
these spirit atoms break into new forms,
invulnerable themselves to all treacherous passages.
. . . We in our raw solitude
accept them.
Listen to clues of old burglaries, to
cracked stones, listen,
castrati sings Mozart,
something about the female gift
some of us have and some imagine.
When lovers have gone we seek escape from newspapers
collapsed in puddles
disintegrating more slowly than the news itself.
We rebel and snarl at brown skies thickening
like butterscotch pudding. Retreat's
not for us;
our coats flap open
as if in spring thaw.

We've come to this café to watch
our thoughts (like etching acid
from batteries left for dead),
dig into brass tables.
We watch the fringes of the tablecloths
unravel to the center
leaving nothing of the last layers
of civilization.
We drink good bitter coffee.

TRACK: A VILLANELLE

The cars geared down and took the turn on two,
"A spinout!" screamed the crowd, then sighed —
I would have hated this if not for you.

Nothing but the sharpest turn would do
as spot to set the ladders, climb astride
watch cars gear down and take the turn on two.

We packed a garbage can with ice and brew
and stood in sun until our brains were fried.
I would have hated this if not for you.

You played we were a Maserati crew
greased and quick, on whom the race relied.
By night we heard each whine and hum as clue.

You told me stories, somehow they seemed true
of how you drove and won and how you cried.
I would have hated this if not for you.

Now —I drive the straight-away as if I flew,
motor roaring, roaring crowd beside,
I gear down take the turn-on too.
How I would have hated this if not for you.

COMMUTER SUNSET

In a long line of cars waiting to get
onto the freeway, I lock up and see the sunset
with its lines of color like a page of
stationery, sentence not formed of letters but

of mango and watermelon colored clouds,
like a love note to raise a sweet fever
on the reader's skin. Behind me, a car honks.
I point up, the driver nods and waves for others

For a few moments, we're all quiet, as our many
pink orange faces turn to the sky.

VI. WAKE

AUBADE

I rise, virtuous at long last, combing earth's hair
before my own, walking into the morning
early as the sun, weaving my way cautiously
between fibrous palms.

Fog heaves off the lake surface, steam rises off
my showered arms.   Like a secret lover's,
my bare feet leave a dark trail
in the grass white with dew shine.

The Lordess, Mother Nature.
is stunned, I'm sure, to have me
join her at this hour, with
my disheveled soul that takes so long to wake.

THE CRONING

The time when there seems to be less, a seed time,
when the sky seems most empty,
when I go out into the trees before dawn,
when I watch a star-filled northern sky
become bleached by the path of the winter moon;
I see the moon sink into the earth

leaving black again; I drink my coffee and brood, as
the blue starts, intensifies to psychic purple, thins to
amethyst, then ghostly grey, a cliché of fear. I rise

to the occasion, raise my cup and throw it, shatter it
against the empty sky. Chips of china fall, like
confetti, like applause.

GENDER SWITCH

The macha winds made
femmey white embroidery
on the lake that was
workshirt blue
this morning.

LESBIAN INDEX

In the savory smells of bacon and muffins,
the news item: lesbians have index fingers
like men's —shorter than ring fingers.

Lying right there beside my pancakes and egg,
beside the newspaper . . . my index finger, short,
shorter than my ring finger, a veritable stub,

unlike my eyebrows whose bushiness is my choice,
my clothes —my jeans, my tailored shirt —this, this is not my choice
but God's will, ha —so after all, I'm innocent.

Shall I make an announcement to the
breakfasters, to the retired couple, and the lawn
worker, the lawyer, and the lawman,

neighbors, servers, one and all
I am a lesbian by nature as well
as nurture? Condemn me not, accept me

into the human family. Shake my lesbian
hand, point out with your respective short and
long fingers, she's okay, just what the plan called for.

ONE AMONG

As my hearing has weakened either from aging or too many rock concerts, and I hear fewer words of songs, as I miss phrases people say and irritate them sometimes in asking them to repeat their words, or in seeming to be utterly oblivious to questions that, in fact, I haven't heard —I miss some softly spoken moments of intimacy, words too shy to speak loudly —the world thus seems to recede from me, withdraws itself somewhat, is a little less affectionate, less at ease with me.

I think of those made suddenly deaf before they have learned sign language to fill their world with communication again. I think of how few of us know sign language.

I remember how I sat an evening at a table of laughing French people and longed to be in on the jokes, how I liked being pulled out of my aloneness by a few English words.

I think of trying to be close to other people at times when I was ashamed of what I was thinking, and the strain of longing to say the unsaid, and how gradually I've learned to disclose more, to admit more, to say no, to say I'm scared, and I'm sorry. And I desire.

And now sometimes a constant frothing forth of intimacies —the waitress bringing a second glass of water, the notches of the Ginkgo tree giving the climber a rough but helpful leg up, a seagull stopping to stare, a sudden glimpse of spirit in a rock —all the touches of any sense, all the day long. A universe of connecting, friends everywhere.

LET

for let us consider the alcoholic
for she leaps into the air
grasping for goddess for she turns
flips rappels cliffs and lands on her feet
many times
for she is determined to win
what she cannot win, the never enough
craving empties her soul
for no one can reach her
for her days peak in two hours
and the rest dwindles into depression
for her will contests windmills
for her ambition engorges
she must fight Goliath
who never plays fair
when she celebrates, she cries later
when she glimpses pride
she knows shame
for her family her friendships
are in tatters
for there is no negotiation
for the plot weaves
no mystery
for the tragic is routine
in a wine-flooded scene

HOW IT FEELS TO BE

quiet like I can't say anything
like I don't know what to say
like I have no hope that anything can be said
like it hasn't rained and won't
like the streets are empty and the traffic
lights are out and it doesn't matter
like I walk down the streets
and I want to go back inside so what
if it's a beautiful day like only
my chair in my room is safe

a great day has dawned, the dawn
of friendship, the end of
marriage, the dawn of respect,
the end of boundary
disputes, the end of a bed I can't
sleep in, the dawn of success at facing fact,
the awakening of realism, the
pink glowing sunrise of alone.

DINNER FOR ONE
from *The Unrequited Crush Papers*

It's not being able to stop yourself from driving down a road
you know is the wrong road, you know by the wide horizon
full of colored light, the trackless dirt road;
it's hearing melodies that aren't there and turning on a radio
to try to quit hearing them. It's a Detroit car lot
shining in a rainy night with flags and reflections in tarmac and prices
miles higher than you can afford.

It's holding an eggplant and gazing with wonder into its dark crystal ball
until you can't cut it, you can't cook it.   Hunger sings,
light switches stick, drawers stick, the olive oil has disappeared.
You are raggedy clothes hanging on a line for all to see,
flapping in the wind, an inexplicable grin.

PATH

to
nowhere —
becomes

the path to now here.

VII. HOMEPORTS

THE SOUTH

Yes, well there's south and south;
there's the collard-greens-
cooked-in-a-wok south,
without pork fat south, the south that
doesn't belong to anyone, especially
those who think they own it,
the south of fountains in the park
and everyone in town knowing about
the one gay boy in white and the six
football linemen, and a video camera that
sees a fountain and sometimes a gray-haired
woman telling stories, but not the linemen
not the gay boy, the southern boy.

There's the south where sand streets in black
neighborhoods act like fog and sweetly
slow the traffic and make the world seem
quiet and full of surprises like vegetable gardens
in the front yard and clothes hanging on fences and
voodoo statues seen through doorways.

The southern towns where on a sunny day
people still take shelter under pink and green
umbrellas as they stroll by Mott's tire store
and Howard Johnson's orange roof and by yards
where people leave sour orange trees alive
for decoration and their fruit lies on the ground
without notice.

The south where a woman stands on the porch
of a beach house, a brow of civilization brooding
on an expanse of ocean where it can't go or can
only go in spirit.

The south of all porches
before air-conditioning, the porches where you
hear your neighbors, and your neighbors might be
the Joneses arguing or it may be Los Angeles
filling a dumpster with paper and looking for
Atlanta to light the match.

The south where metal racks of brochures
of the Chamber of Commerce advertise the
Bible Belt—Forbidden Caverns,
the Cave of the Four Gospels. "See the holy city
built entirely out of bottle caps."

See the bridge where Dr. King led a march into
the mouths of police dogs and under the hooves
of police horses, where the ankles and wrists
of a woman twisted in the hands of police and
the loose collar of her blue dress dragged
in the street.

Yes, it's the south where churches have
long names —the Temple of the Washed Sanctified and
Redeemed Singing Together into Glory
Brotherhood and Sisterhood church. Where churches
buckle the belts of the empty two-lane
roads that wind through flooded fields
with bits of cotton clinging to barbed wire and bracken.

The south where the Klan set a burning cross
in the yard of the house
that Frank Lloyd Wright designed, and where the Rosenbaums
had a party that night anyway
and teenagers kept up their courage by singing
Peter, Paul, and Mary songs, and it seemed that everyone
got drunk, some for the first time, and these
nights may have gotten compressed by story-telling,

but the next week we took down signs that said
colored and white and someone put
them back up again, and again we took them down,
and on and on, until now
the only ones left are invisible.

It's the south where you can pick up
shells on the barrier reefs to put on
dashboards of Volkswagen vans and where
you can pick up both Canadian newspapers and
boxes of grits at the Handyway and where you
can pick up bits of African patois that forms
the basic dialects of both the
Georgia Sea Islands and the
drawing rooms of Savannah bankers.

There's the new version of southern hospitality,
the underground sanctuary movement
hiding children from the perpetrators of their rapes.
from the law that gave the perpetrators custody.
Black and white women together
doctors' wives, house-workers, lawyers
join to pass out leaflets,
flood over the streets,
young flaring with fury, the silver-haired
old a tidal wave of raging whitecaps,
the once binding proprieties of southern women
now wielded as weapons of defiance
of their own men —the judges and sheriffs —
their sons, husbands, and brothers.

"This is Mississippi?" asks Oprah, dumbfounded,
(she grew up there); yes, these ladies picketing
the Hattiesburg jail, yes these once silenced women
passing out leaflets that report the torn hymen
of a four-year-old girl ladies coming out
publicly, breaking the taboos, telling the secrets.

This is the south, the mellifluous accents
interviewed now in Boston, and
San Francisco and Washington. No sir,
we won't leave this child unbefriended, the song
of the Delta spreading across the world—
the Harrisons, the Singleys, Chrissy Foxworth,
the Newsoms. "Who hid this girl?" asked the judge,
and voices all over the Delta and Gulf Coast said
"I did, I did, Yes sir, I did."

And if some of these ladies
hurt their own children
let that be said,
and if anyone be
unjustly accused
let that be said, and of those who
were hurt in their childhoods,
let that be told.

To be sure, that's the south,
yes ma'am, yes ma'am!
The south of the African-American Festival,
of the Yoruba ceremony on the stage of the
university, where Winnie Mandela speaks
and feels right at home she says,
where there's Fanny Lou Hamer Day, and
the Klan Watch and
the Southern Poverty Law Center
and the Center for Democratic Renewal
and people hanging up signs
in their windows, a black hand and a white hand,
clasped in a handshake: "Hate Free Zone."

There's the south of the W.C. Handy Festival,
the cake walk, the jazz music the whites in town
are just lately proud of, that south.
And next door, the still segregated south,
where some doctors receive patients from separate
waiting rooms. Such last doctors are rare now,
rare and bloody as a steak
charcoaled that smells up a city block with
burning flesh lit with lighter fluid.

It's the fluid south, the changing turquoise rivers
that were the sliding roads of Indians,
secured now by routed wood signs,
the last sanctuaries of wilderness, where public
access signs mark the dead-end streets of the southern
beaches, the tender weed-sweetened cracks between
mammoth condominiums with guards
at the gates.

The now-no-one's-from-the-south-south
and people miss the Vermont seasons
and remember snow and think
they still need four-wheel drive
for the snowy white sand. That's the
people-seasoning-grits-with-tamari-south.

Now the magnolia blossoms
over people chewing peyote buttons,
and the good weather brings BMWs and Monte Carlos
and the homeless.

Now the salt water tosses
in the southern surf and a lesbian
community of thirteen homes celebrates
its thirteenth year.

Now on a coral reef nestling
under the banana trees
there's a center for the study of nonviolent
civil disobedience. Now Robert E. Lee has
been kicked out of the office of model southern
gentleman and Bill Maxwell has been elected.
Now there's a town named Casa Dega,
place of God, where northern spiritualists
came and stayed, where today you can get a room with
a porch and a psychic reading.

Now still, dolphins swim in
perfect curves, making blessings up and down
the coast. Now still there's
the y'all-come-on-over south, the slow
southern drawl, the palmettos prickling
the southern air; and there's
the south with an itch,
the south where visionaries move to
pare down a beginning dream of paradise to
more skin in the wind, the south where
vision can begin again.

AT THE RIVER RISE

the river mirror makes two of everything
and two makes one
the white egret's long neck curves down
the river mirror neck curves up to make one circle

the roots of the cypress trees along the banks hang visible
in this time of low water
the river mirror offers them back long lost sister roots
relatives unseen in years

the fish bouncing across the surface of the water
like a skipping stone
meets a playful fellow from underneath in the same
touching and arches

the eye of the owl at sunset creeps open to see
deep down in the river mirror an owl waking
here for you I give you your past,
your days in nature,

your memories of sweet gum and maple
black water and kingfisher.
I give you the southern swamp
your memories match every palmetto

match every big blue heron with feathery beard
every egret that flies ahead and lands on
a green island of pond lily then looks back
to see if you are coming along.

SOUTHERN HEARTBREAK

Watermelon heart
break open;
give your red pulp
your potent black seeds.

Peach heart
break open; don't worry!
Furry skin on forearm and leg
cheek and neck
remember the touches.

Sky heart, go on,
break open; embrace
continents when
your lover leaves.

SWIMMING IN THE VOID

for J. Hahn

Many a love that I have had
I lost,
gone to memory, gone
to wind, gone to
other arms
or death; and simpler loves
went too—a matched pair
of painted plates, a pleated skirt,
an English bike, songs not
written down.

When I dive in the deep of that
dark chest that engulfs
joys I want to store,
grasping won't work—
skin falls off the bones, words
melt, there's no trace of steps.
no line to climb back to the surface,
in that cavern of skies
where new clouds arrive
from nowhere
behind the moon of that night.

OLD HOMEPLACE

We pick our way around the outside of
the old house, setting foot deliberately so as
not to trip in the tangle of vines, planted
no longer by anything but fairies, or ghosts of
moms and dads.

We cautiously touch sills of windows,
porches of spiders, peeking through slats into rooms
now empty and spacious, finally uncluttered.
We remember beds here, faces, armed words, steamed
windows. A safe retreat that turned into a cave
with us wanting to leave for a garden.

No one inside now sees how the night lights
grew and daylight retreated into a few hours,
how the family disappeared, one by one, leaving
aromas, echoes, then nothing.

This shell was our home,
a carapace for a child's biology collection,
a dollhouse for dreams and nightmares.

We grew up, became gamblers, we
shook the house like dice, rolled it on the green,
counted its dark windows, shattered the lie of the white
    metal columns,
and won the time to go.

THOSE FIRST DAYS

Watching you on the pillow
hair flying, mouth pulled to one side,
the look in your eyes as you try
by the force of your will
to communicate thoughts without
the words you've forgotten. When
your mouth opens, it's disconnected from
the words you're trying to form,
speaks its own crazed language
of metaphors and made-up words and
sudden familiar phrases that appear and disappear
into a surf of tossing tumult. Watching you
I say, "Mother, I hear you, I understand."

DAISIES OF THE ANCESTORS

My mom and dad were daisies —
Me'n my brother would pull the petals, he loves me,
she don't, she'll parent me, he won't. Discouraged,
my brother decided to race chariots instead of, you know,
like get married, and have kids, which was okay
until his girlfriend had a green and yellow iguana with
little erections running down his back, and she was
scared to be alone with it. My brother, he smelled
a song coming on, a song of garlic and basil and of course
rosemary, so I married music, but it was clear from
my brother's child, we had amphibians and dragons
in our ancestry, at least frogs, and we would
hop around the living room in front of visitors.
Nous sommes descendons de les dragons,
growling the French *r*, the groping croakers
of siblinghood, pure-voiced as the swamp.

We're frog princes, I proclaim, triumphant as Alexander.

Like jump ropes our vision lines turn and
cross each other before the retina; everything's
actually upside down, or sometimes, writing lines
stretch from tree to tree and we balance on them;
we tie them to the horses and pull our chariots with them.
This is now and forever, our bloodline
(unless you would call an iguana an exception,
which I would not). Pulled by dual forces of
shame and pride, fresh spinach and bent cans, someday

We will emerge, dazed as Ezekiel at the Golden Gate place
where charioteers wear flowers in their hair. You laugh,
but you will see us, you will sing with us, you will
remember the garlic words as we say them,
remember the French and Italian, the tattoos of Thailand,
the daisies with North African roots. Our

Ancestors will ascend together like angels, gamboling like
lambs on some sunny rock in the Aegean, looking back to
the first daisy, back to the first line cast in the sea,
the first wet fish to walk ashore.

THE JACKET

For weeks it was lost
and I looked for it,
drove to store after store
to school and office, none of which
I had business with, just wondering if
I had left it there —a strange journey.
I slowed down without purchase,
waiting for managers.
In a foyer on a stool in Leonardo's
I watched pizzas pass by with anchovies
and pineapple and grouper
watched people come in
suspecting them of taking my jacket
unable to resist its softness
its coolness, the slick inside pocket.
I looked at backs and shoulders
with new interest.

I went to the Hippodrome where the lost and found box
is on the third floor
where the cast was dressing
people in ruffled shirts, gluing on beards,
holding up hoopskirts over pantaloons.

I'm sure I looked lonely on my pilgrimage of
lost and founds,
and I wondered if I were the only one alone, if I
made people uncomfortable
made them think about divorce or rejection;
was I bringing them down? Were they
saying look at that lonely person, no
don't look. I was
like a person missing an ear or
the left side of the body.

In my eyes I am only missing
a jacket
its soft arms that
slip around mine with
inner satin that touches my skin.
People hug me,
Um, nice jacket they say
I am cool and confident in it.

Now I'm my own Sherlock
tracing myself.
Where was I that day,
then where did I go?

In one lost and found box
I found a sweater I had left
another year
when I was tired of it.
Here it is now,
no one needed it so I'll
take the sweater back.
I'll take it to the nursing home.
Mother is often cold now,
I take her sweater after
sweater and long socks and
afghans and flannel pajamas.
She doesn't know who I am
at first, but I make the connection
and she lights up.
I will lose her soon, her hugs,
her bony hand to hold.
So I want to find
my jacket.

MY BROTHER

Where, Bob, have you been,
traveling in your mind, you
who dropped out of
work life twenty years ago,
who stayed at home since then,
only going out to the doctor
for checkups, for medicine?

Where are you, Bob?
Are you in your body
long wracked by illness you are
healing from?

Are you in the place where you see
Jesus and the Eckmaster and Mataji and
Yogi Paramahansa Yogananda?

"Come outside," I say,
sit by the ocean with me.
"No, you go," you say, "Enjoy, say hello
to your goddess in the sea."

Daily, Bob, you feed the birds,
daily spray the plants,
twice daily meditate,
cook meals exactly to a plan,
three times a day
test your blood sugar. "You're
doing great, Bob," I say,
and you return the praise.
You think I'm getting kinder.

Today
as you left the living room after meditating,
Mother whispered to me,
"He's doing so much better these days."
"I wish he had stayed to talk," I said.
"He'll be back," Mother said,
"He's brushed my hair
ever since I had a stroke," and
she was right. You
came back, leaned over her
tenderly and gallantly
as she sat on the couch.
"You're looking beautiful
this morning, Mother," you said.
(Indeed she was.) Then with one hand
you carefully moved a brush
over her white head,
while with a comb in your other hand
you made a part, your touch
weightless and silken as her hair.

Where are you, Bob, in a world
where kindness reigns supreme,
where people see with spirit's eyes?
With your schizophrenia
and Mother's dementia,
you learned how to take care
of heads that bleed easily.

TOUCH

when talk is gone, once again
all is touch
in the final months
all of the beloved is precious, wrinkled skin,
sagging jowls, or balls, or beautiful face,
the grey in hair and face
the softness of skin sliding above
the remains of muscles

holy one precious one dearly loved one
I would touch these thin transparent hands
these soft lost muscles
any part
would be joy to touch
my heart as opened as a young lover
more
my heart more opened than a young lover
I have reached beyond
anger beyond desire
you have so little left of you
that superficial
only the heart is left
it greets my heart
only the ferocious love
is left, only
the blessing touch tiptoeing over my face
your frail
eloquent fingers

even with
the smell of piss the ache
the awe of death, the lips that refuse food
the spirit claiming its destiny
the hour of vigil, the slow breaths,
the unbeliever sitting in miracle
we are very together here
and we are very alone
each of us
finally sure
this is love.

ABOUT THE AUTHOR

Kathleen Culver lives in a log cabin on a lake with eagles, egrets, herons, and her cat, Pele. Her life has always been stimulated by writing and language; her mother was an English teacher, her father a poet.

Culver has a Ph.D. in English and American Literature, writing both her Master's thesis and Ph.D. dissertation on Henry David Thoreau. She taught English at the University of Florida, the University of North Florida, and Santa Fe Community College.

Active in her community in support of the environment, the arts, feminism, and peace, Culver also enjoys camping, hiking, kayaking, dancing, and playing music with her friends.

www.ingramcontent.com/pod-product-compliance
Lightning Source LLC
La Vergne TN
LVHW090047090426
835511LV00031B/346